Where Do Plants and Animals Live?

HOUGHTON MIFFLIN HARCOURT

PHOTOGRAPHY CREDITS: (c) ©Thomas Kitchin & Victoria Hurst/Canopy/Corbis; 3 (b) ©kaphotokevm1/Fotolia; 4 (c) ©Getty Images Royalty Free; 6 (l) Greg Dale/National Geographic/Getty Images; 6 (r) ©Radius/SuperStock; 7 (l) ©Radius Images/Alamy Images; 7 (r) Getty Images/Photodisc; 9 (t) ©Thomas Kitchin & Victoria Hurst/Canopy/Corbis; 10 (l) ©Getty Images; 10 (r) ©Steve Klics/Fancy/Corbis; 11 (l) ©Photodisc/Getty Images; 11 (c) © BYphoto / Alamy; 11 (r) ©Corbis

Printed in China

ISBN: 978-0-544-07215-2

11 12 13 14 0940 20 19 18 17

4500693646 A B C D E F G

Be an Active Reader!

Look for each word in yellow along with its meaning.

living things	environment
reproduce	shelter
nonliving things	food chain

Underlined sentences answer these questions.

What are living things?

What are nonliving things?

What is an environment?

Where do plants and animals live?

How do plants and animals get food?

What is a food chain?

What are living things?

Living things are plants, animals, and people. They need food, air, and water.

Living things reproduce. They make young that look like themselves.

This mother lion has reproduced.

What are nonliving things?

Nonliving things do not need food and water to live. They do not need air and space to live. Nonliving things do not make new living things like themselves.

Rocks are nonliving things.

What is an environment?

An environment is all the living and nonliving things in a place.

This is a terrarium. It is an environment.

This turtle will use things in its environment.

Where do plants and animals live?

Plants live in different environments. A forest is one place where plants grow. It usually gets a lot of rain. A desert is another place where plants grow. Deserts are dry. They can be hot.

A forest can have tall trees.

A cactus is a desert plant.

Some birds build nests for shelter.

Fish live in water.

Animals live in different environments. Animals can live on land, in water, or in both places.

Many animals use plants for a shelter. A shelter is a place where an animal can be safe. Birds use trees as a shelter.

How do plants and animals get food?

All living things need food. A plant makes its own food. It uses sunlight to make food. The roots take in water.

Black bears eat plants and animals.

Many animals eat plants. Many animals eat meat. Some animals eat both plants and animals.

What is a food chain?

Plants and animals need one another to live. A food chain shows how energy moves from plants to animals.

A plant makes food from sunlight.

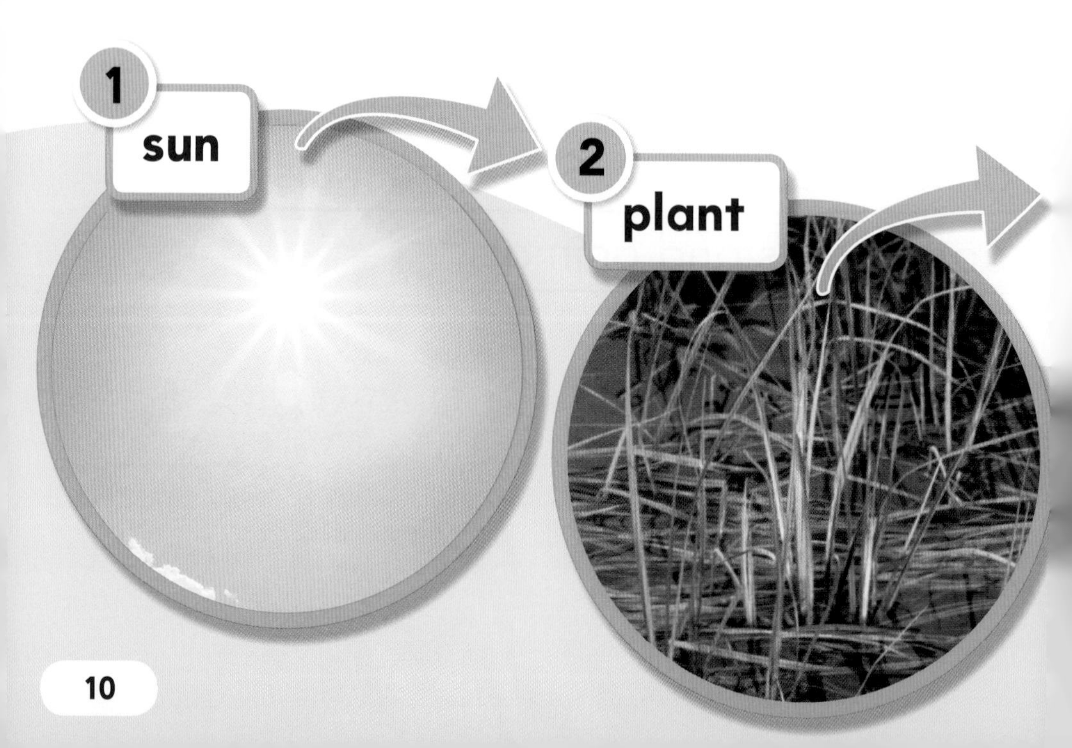

An insect eats a plant. A small animal eats the insect. A larger animal eats the smaller animal.

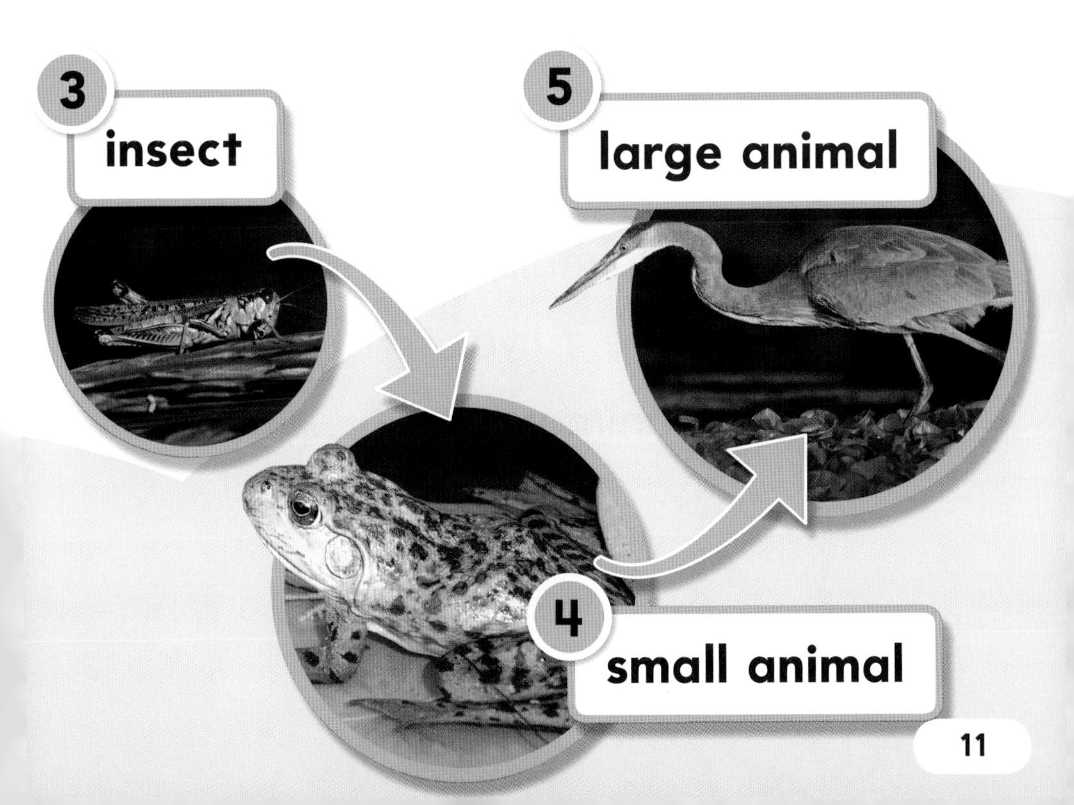

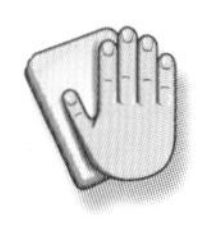

Sort the Pictures

Work with a partner. Cut out magazine pictures of living and nonliving things. Label each picture. Sort the pictures by living things and nonliving things.

Write a Sentence

Work with a partner. Read a book about an animal you like. Write about where it lives. Write about what the animal eats.